solidago
literary journal

WINTER 2018

INITIATION

5th April 2019

FOUNDING EDITORS

CATHERINE BRERETON

SUSAN STEWART

KOPANA TERRY

INTERN

SABRINA SMITH

www.solidagojournal.com

CONTENTS

ART

FICTION

NONFICTION

POETRY

SOLIDAGO
JOURNAL

WINTER 2018

INITIATION

From the beginning, please.

My mother told me she loved me
with Christmas sweaters in July.

I am throwing her ashes out to sea,
but the wind keeps sending her back.

I remember Leila. Did she find
what she was looking for? he asks,
making notes on how I hold my hands.

Listless as ever, I change the subject
and tell him that I micro dosed molly
at a Latin club last night just to feel
a little more lotus and a lot less mud.

The comedown was a real sonofabitch,
but it helped me hang onto the ribbon
threaded through my brain, in one ear
and out the other, dredging up childhood
when a guy in another blue button down
asked me to dance, his smile gin-certain;

I wanted to know if he had an MBA.
He did, and I said, Color me surprised.
I'd rather color you mauve.
I couldn't decide if this was a come on.

There's a box of tissues on the table
that my fingers make short work of,
strip after strip. I want to make myself
scarce. He's a pendulum. My ribs are
constricting then expanding out larger;
there's not enough room, so I let it out:

Do you think Lazarus's resurrection
made him happy? Or did he spend the rest
of his preternatural life trying to get home?
Suicide is a sin, you know; death, a sacrament.

Do you still have the sweaters?

BAILEY A
MERLIN

**IN CONVERSATION
WITH YET ANOTHER
THERAPIST I
STOPPED SEEING**

1

Of course I do but don't admit that I've unraveled
them into piles of knots that are hidden in my house.
They didn't fit me anymore. *Maybe it's time
to give them away.* His words linger there,
ash in the wind, blowing back into my face.

SOLIDAGO
JOURNAL

WINTER 2018

INITIATION

The landlady opened the door. A wave of musty air preceding her.

You'll be down for the funeral then?

He took off his hat. I am.

A thin hand ushering him into the dark hallway. Come through. You'll have tea?

I will.

She put the kettle on the hob and coughed once. It's a long way down from Dublin, she said.

It is, he said. *Seven hours. Waiting at some godforsaken siding on the edge of a bog for two hours. Nothing to read and only a gaggle of bleeding nuns for company. Thinking about her laid out on a cooling board. And whether or not they'd have the silver pieces on her closed eyes yet.*

The landlady dribbled tea into his chipped cup. Her own no better.

And will there be more of ye?

There will, yes. Comin in on the ferry I think. Is it far from the village?

No, no, she said. A good country mile. You'd walk it easy. She coughed again. It's to rain agin tonight.

The weather. The interminable fuckin weather. And always the fuckin rain. Coming down to oppress the bleedin life out of every last one of ye, keep ye beholdin and ever watchful of any change, wax or wane, shackled to it like nothing better than a beast.

***

And now here comes this gobshite trying to pat me arse before I can escape. And his wife a sour ould prune of a bitch down in her cabin.

Good evening Maureen.

She turned smiling. A huge and false smile. Mister Kilmurray. How's your missus? Still suffering, the poor divil?

And now her grin was real as his face blanched like it always did when she mentioned his wife. *He only ever wants the ladies to bring something else up.*

STEPHEN
O'DONNELL

HOMEKEEPING

5

Manky bastard. Jaysus Christ imagine letting him on top of you. The googly fucking eyes on him.

Oh much the same, he muttered. Much the same. A hint of rum on his breath already.

Give her my best will you, and tell her I was asking for her? You'll excuse me running off on you but I've left me earrings in the cabin.

She turned and fled from whatever it was he rasped after her. Feeling his eyes like candleflames on her rump. *A friend of your daddy alright. Dipso bastard.*

The steward wiped his face with his handkerchief and then he lifted both bags and set off down the gangplank. She followed him closely. *Cant be too careful with these young lads. Be only too happy to go through your unmentionables for a thrill. He's not much to look at but you never can tell. Not until you have them kneeling naked before you begging with their brains out.*

The lights of a motor car peeled across the wet wharf and she drew the weathered stole around her. *Will they all be here yet?* and breathing seaweed and turfsmoke above the wet stone of the pier she thought of her mother *dead now and walled from this world forever and the lack of her like a pit within me deepening and deepening.* She heard Kilmurray muttering on the gangplank behind her and she followed after the steward toward the customs office.

As the cab jolted over the level crossing she watched the dock recede through the rear windscreen. The ferry lit up like a carnival, steaming slowly back out to the open sea. Solid in the water, trailing a faint vapour of grey smoke that curled slowly from a single stack.

* * *

He shouldered his way gently through the knots of men. Talking, jeering, wheedling each other between sups. A god awful stench of piss on dripstoned piss. Sawdust pasted to the toe of his brogues.

Sorry there, sorry lads, excuse me, cheers.

Men glancing at him as each group parted until he stood in the general chaos of the bar.

Stout, he told the landlady. He looked down the line of ruddy faced farmers. A tide of worn knuckles and cheeks shaved raw for the mass.

Bobbing hats and Sunday grey overcoats and a noise to raise the dead. Talking weather, beef and milk, how much and what price. Cultivators and drays. He didn't recognise any of their faces.

The landlady set his pint down and hovered before him until he noticed her and handed over a wad of sweaty coins. Absently patting the billfold in his chestpocket *yer a long way from those Dublin lurchers bai.*

He took a few slow sips and then he edged his way back toward the wall. He stood the glass on the wooden rail and rolled a cigarette.

He was standing there smoking, trading coarse jokes with a booster, when she walked in the door.

The entire room silenced in an instant. All eyes were on her. The booster was mid sentence when he saw her.

The booster nudged him. Here's trouble.

Already she was beside him. There you are and for godssakes will you get out of this bloody place. You've a hundred and one bloody things to do.

Someone heckled him from the bar. Go on bai better do as yer told. Laughter.

Could you not have sent a boy in for me, he hissed. Jesus Christ you're not on the bloody Riviera now. He turned to roll his eyes at the booster, as if to say *do you see what is put upon me* but the man had abandoned him.

I'll finish this and be out, he said and then he turned his back to her.

* * *

You're not down an hour and you're drinking and laughing with the lads.

I was having one bloody pint.

You're not on your fucking holidays Sheamy. You're here to bury your bloody mother.

What haven't I arranged?

So you sent a few telegrams and a long distance call and that's it, time to get locked?

7

For the love of God, I was only having the one.

Having the one. She smiled callously at him. You were only having that one and the next one and then next one. God knows what state the other one will turn up in, I need you to be bloody sober.

In case what?

In case she does what she always does and goes off like usual and makes every last damned thing about her. She nurses her slights, she'll have been feeding them since she first heard about mama.

Ah for Jaysus sake, is that the way you're thinking already?

That'll be the bloody way of it. You know how she is. She'll be making a show of herself before the first clod is down.

Ah stop it for fucks sake. You haven't seen each other in years.

I know that. Who's fault is that?

Jesus Christ, he said. You're here for mama. Can you not be civil?

I'll be civil Sheamy. But I can promise you this now, she wont be fucking civil. There's nothing civil about that bitch.

That's your sister you're talking about. That's your blood.

If bread can be a body, she can be me sister and still be a thunderin fuckin bitch.

* * *

The undertaker now stepping across the threshold wearing a look of apologetic collusion. *Come to peddle the same sympathy he sells them all.* Not a big man, hair clipped close and not a thing out of place, nothing unusual or upsetting in his dress or his composure. He baled out his condolences and then he turned down the tea offered by the landlady.

No, thank you missus, I'm alright.

The landlady nodded and made a great show of leaving and drawing shut the door behind her. *She'll nail her ear to that door and half the bleedin village will know the lot before the hours out.*

It's just the two of ye down so far?

It is, there's a gang more due on this evenings train.

The undertaker had lifted a pocketwatch from inside his waistcoat. That'd usually be quite late getting in.

That's fine, the man said. He glanced at his sister. We can go ahead without her?

We can, Maureen said.

Well, said the undertaker. My lads have the plot ready.

His sister smiled appreciatively. Thank you. That will have been hard work in the rain.

Ah yeah, hard work in the rain, like he isn't making a shilling out of it. Probably dug by rubes who don't know enough to even think to ask for a cut.

It's nothing we haven't done before. Down here we'd be in trouble if the rain stopped. He pressed his palms together. Now, as regards a coffin, have you any thoughts or special requests?

Sheamy, what do you think?

Nothing too ostentatious, he warned.

No, no, his sister repeated. Mama wouldn't like any fuss.

That's fine, we have some rather restrained pine pieces. Simple. Tasteful.

Tasteful, fine. *Leave me to rot in a ditch were her words. If she could've heard how much this bastard quoted me.*

The undertaker leaned back and adjusted the cuffs of his shirt. I've spoken to the priest and the mass has been arranged. The priest will of course need his due.

Of course, Sheamy said. *Not even the dead can rest without their dues paid. Four fingers in every piece from here to the holy see.*

Were there any other requests she might have had?

Silver pieces. Over her eyes.

9

Oh yes, his sister said. I had forgotten.

She had a fondness for the old ways.

That's no problem, the undertaker said.

Now, will you have a drop of port for the road?

No thank you ma'am, I had best be home before my dinner is cold. He stood up and shook their hands. Then as he touched the doorhandle to leave he turned back.

As if he had forgot. As if he forgot me hole.

When you're ready a gravestone will need to be chosen.

Yes of course, Maureen said.

And lastly of course there is the cost to be settled with the parlour.

His sister nodded solemnly. Of course, of course. Sheamy you have your chequebook there, don't you?

He looked at her, in her silk blouse and her pinned hat and her eyes on him unwavering and then he nodded quickly and reached for his over coat where it hung from the back of the chair. He scribbled out the cheque quickly. That'll cover everything so far, he said.

The undertaker took the cheque from him, read it and then folded it reverently and placed it into his pocket. Good evening now, he said.

A good evening alright. He's not worried about his fucking dinner anymore.

* * *

She had arrived in Dublin on the early ferry and she had been drinking since the train station. The children were quiet now, dozing in their seats. Nodding and shifting when the carriage rocked on the tracks, when the brakes whistled like bottle rockets.

From behind his newspaper her husband said: God only knows who's idea it was for an express train to stop at every blasted station on the line. Wasn't our lot you can be bloody sure.

She nodded absently. She was thirsty for water but the dining cart was

so far away that she just had another sip from the flask. *I'm not so bad now they won't notice and sure if they do amn't I entitled to a thimbleful from time to time when I'm only home now and then sure Christ himself knows they couldn't begrudge it I know they wouldn't especially not now with poor mammy O mama o mama* and she stifled a sob that racked her until she belched.

One of the children stirred at this, and sniffing the air, began to cry.

Now you've done it, her husband hissed at her. Now you bloody well have, you drunken bitch.

But she was not listening, she was watching the countryside pass and remembering bicycling down narrow lanes with schoolfriends, gossiping and laughing in the sea breeze, remembering starlight over open fields arm in arm with lean young lovers. Baking bread in the old farmhouse kitchen with her mother. *O mama O mama.* And now she seemed to hear the cries of the child for the first time and she lifted the child into her arms.

Don'sh cry poppet. Shhhh. Don'sh cry. Granmamas only sleeping.

Her husband lowered his broadsheet. She's crying because you're breathing a bathtub of bloody gin down her throat.

She clutched the child tight and rocked her. Listen to the big teetotaller. Lisssten. She's missing her gram gram, aren'sh you poppet? Shh now. Shhhh.

Slowly she laid the child back in the seat and staggered back to her seat. She fumbled with the flask. She had difficulty opening the cap.

For god's sake, her husband muttered.

She persevered and took another neat mouthful. Just enough to deaden the passing of the forlorn countryside beyond the window.

The train pulled into the station after midnight. Her husband had arranged for a cab to be waiting for them. She was hardly able to stand.

The driver rolled down his window and nodded. A soft day for the parish sir.

Indeed, her husband said. I daresay you know where it is you're to take us?

Only if you have the address sir?

My God man. I was assured by that bloody booking agent.

Well sir I cant find a place if I'm not even told the name, can I?

Just a moment. Blasted unreliable agent. He lifted the two children and laid them snug into the backseat. When he turned back to her she was lying flat on the pavement, singing unintelligibly, oblivious to the rain. He pulled her to her feet and lugged her around to the far door and pushed her roughly inside. Then he climbed into the passenger seat and handed the address for the drive.

Bit the worse for the wear, is she sir? the driver chirped as they swung out onto the main road.

Drive the bloody car. Can't you see she's grieving?

Oh yes sir. I see that, the driver said. Yous will be down for the funeral then?

Why the hell else would we be in a boil of place like this, except to bury the dead? Now just do what I'm paying you to do and drive the blasted car.

* * *

He woke to the wailing of children beneath him. *So they've arrived.* He got up and took his time washing and shaving as the wailing continued unabated. He heard a door open and a man speaking soothingly to the child.

He moved down the staircase unhurriedly and a small child ran to his shin and blubbered up at him.

Dada, Dada.

I'm not your Dada, he laughed and patted her head.

The child looked up at strange voice and then she began to wail.

Jesus bloody Christ what in the hell is it now? Oh hello Seamus. Wondered what'd set her off again. Well girl, say hello to your uncle.

Hello Rodney, Sheamy said and he picked the child up. Lets have a

look at you then. Which one are you?

Susie, the child blubbered.

You're not Susie. Susie's a baby.

Am too.

Are you now? Tell me Susie are you fond of sweeties?

The child nodded shyly.

You're not? I'll have to find another little girl to give them to them.

I am I am.

Ah well that's good now because I've a few pennies for you then. He rattled his pocket. I don't think you'd want them though, would you?

She nodded again.

Hold up your hand so.

She held out her hand and he passed her a few pennies. Buy yourself a hot air balloon. He set her down and she scurried off giggling.

How was the train down?

Bloody awful. Might as well have been going backward.

Well you're here now. Mary awake?

No, not yet. She'll be up and on the warpath soon enough.

I don't doubt it, Sheamy said. If I make tea will you have a cup?

I will, thank you.

* * *

She slept and dreamt of rats, trapped and scratching behind the wall, multiplying in a frantic tide along the innards of the house. Multiplying until the plaster seams burst and they swarmed in a tide of teeth and feverish eyes that woke her screaming and drenched in sweat.

She's awake then, Maureen said.

Sheamy's eyes met hers. He shook his head.

They were in the drawing room, lounging in deep, dusty chairs.

Rodney put his paper on his knee. Susie, he called. Susie. Bring mama some water. Fetch a glass. Good girl.

A sound of glass smashing in the kitchen. The child roaring. Rodney leapt from his chair and ran into the kitchen, pages of his paper scattering in his wake.

Sheamy slapped his sister's knee. Get a clamp on that vipers tongue of yours. Christ.

* * *

He cut several strips of fatty rashers and used one to grease the pan.

And Maureen had only turned from the sink when the other one said it. You weren't fucking there when I asked you to be, at your own nieces baptism.

Maureen slapped the dishrag into the sink. What? What'd you say?

And Sheamy among them now as the greast spat in the skillet. Don't, don't, for gods sake don't, not today. Of all days.

Did you tell him you spoke to that solicitor before you came home? Did you?

Can you not let me alone to grieve, can you not let me alone to do that? You're no more here for mama than a stranger. You've come to drown yourself in wine.

Oh shut up Maureen. Do you have to make every little thing into a pantomime? Hold that righteous mirror up to yourself some time.

Piety, piety is what you need. You're supposed to be raising children, all you raise is a bottle.

Such fine clothes, how much choking did that cost you?

Jaysus, Sheamy shouted, Jaysus fucking Christ. Stop it will you? For

jaysus sake.

They fumed in silence. Sheamy sank into his chair.

These eggs are splendid, Rodney said.

Where do they learn their manners? You wouldn't think they had it in them to subjugate half the fucking world. Yeah, Sheamy murmured. Yeah.

* * *

And what nameless day is this? Now see the casket in the rented room of a strangers house. Three pounds a night. Cold silver pieces across her colder eyes. A bottle of bushmills in every corner.

Oh indeed it is hard work, the hardest work to carry it up to the graveyard, the priest told the landlady. Especially in this rain. But the dead have to be buried.

SOLIDAGO
JOURNAL

WINTER 2018

INITIATION

He directs her to take turn after turn until she no longer knows where she is. The houses on the street look familiar, but not. Streetlamps are the only light. The night is purple and full of shadows.

When he points to the place, Lillie parks on the street. They get out and walk through a gate, between little houses that seem to be sinking into the ground. Under an aluminum awning, they go in the backdoor of a house with uneven floors. Lillie doesn't know why they're here. Jay gave a flimsy excuse that sounded like a lie and now here they are.

The house is full of people, but they're all quiet. Sitting on the floor, standing in corners, and perched on dingy brown furniture, they don't even notice as Lillie follows Jay through hallways and nearly empty bedrooms, down a step here, up one there. She looks around at the wood paneled walls, the ripped linoleum floors, and the film of dirt and cigarette ash settled on everything.

Then she realizes she's alone. She doesn't know where Jay went. She searches for him, looking sheepishly into the faces of strangers. They're not yet married, but it feels like there's no turning back. Her father has already said, "It's me or him," and she made her choice. Lillie is nineteen years old and thinks this man is all she has in the world.

It's like running into an invisible wall when what smells like burning plastic enters her lungs and clings to her hair, her clothes. There he is, sitting on the arm of a couch next to a friend of his. He brings a metal pipe to his mouth. Lillie's never seen hard drugs before. The danger feels palpable. When he smiles, Jay's teeth are gleaming and Lillie wishes she could crawl out of her skin and disappear. As he laughs and she stands alone and afraid, she knows he has no desire to protect her from anything. No one can protect her anymore.

Lillie feels like she's suspended by a string, dangling over a fire that smells like burning tires. She knows they could be here for hours because Jay doesn't care to make her wait. If she wants to be with him, he reasons, she'll wait until he's ready to leave. Lillie has no idea if secondhand crack smoke is dangerous or how likely it is that police will bust in any minute.

Her fear and his indifference is enough to propel her body through the house. As if in a fog, she's guided only by one step after another. She starts the car and drives before she knows where she's going. She can't remember

AMANDA
KELLEY
CORBIN

**FEAR
AND
INDIFFERENCE**

17

how she got here. After a few blocks, she comes to a street she's traveled countless times before. In the rearview is a world she hadn't known existed. The farther she drives, the darker the neighborhood in the mirror looks, the color disappearing like skintone under a bruise.

SOLIDAGO
JOURNAL

WINTER 2018

INITIATION

What is something said
if I want to change the world

in my direction? Do me a favor
and ask what can I get you.

Be kind to me and I will be there
for me. I give myself a little credit.

Who am I calling little?
I get this body to sink as I please

in an ocean of bleached teeth,
my luxury yacht of skin.

Link your pinky finger on mine.
Kiss your thumb in your mouth

and swear like a sailor. We got a deal.
Thank you. I want the world

to end with me in it,
smoke amok, no takesy-backsies.

I hate to see anyone going on
without me. My pickled tail,

its vinegary legacy. Forever.
I take comfort in

by brute force. And ever.

HENRY
GOLDKAMP

MAN POEM

SOLIDAGO
JOURNAL

WINTER 2018

INITIATION

By a miracle of God or perhaps only sloppy paperwork, I was placed in the bunkhouse with the older girls.

There were six of them—all at least 15, all *real teenagers,* in my eyes. I didn't remember all of their names, except for Roxanne, who seemed to be the clear leader of the group. They wore two-toned jeans and high tops with slouch socks. When they thought they could get away with it, they also wore off-the-shoulder tops they slid back up to their necks when the counselors were watching and miniskirts they tried to tug to their knees before they were instructed to go back to the bunkhouse to change. They teased their hair high with White Rain hairspray and spritzed Blue Jeans perfume on their wrists and the back of their ears. They wore blue mascara and bold lipstick, and, sometimes, their bra straps slipped into view before—with the frown of the preacher—they were tucked back away.

But they were more than just clothes. They *knew* things. They *knew* how to climb in and out of the bunkhouse windows to meet boys without getting caught. They *knew* where the camp counselors had their nightly meetings. They *knew* where they could sneak smokes—as they called the contraband cigarettes they somehow possessed—and how to use baby powder to get rid of the smell that lingered on their clothes.

I was not yet 12 that summer. I was fascinated.

For years, I had spent part of my summer vacation at Camp Christian, a retreat tucked deep in the Laurel Mountains of Pennsylvania about three hours from my home. It was a place dedicated to summer fun: swimming, hiking, and cooking outside. And of course, as the name suggested, the site was a religious camp, dedicated to the worship of God and to general Christian fellowship.

In other words, the world of the typical 80's teenager was to be left outside the camp grounds. We were not supposed to listen to music except for Christian Rock. We were supposed to wear appropriate and modest clothing. And of course, there was no fraternizing with the opposite sex.

The girls in my bunkhouse ignored all of these rules.

Most of the time they also ignored me. I was simply a cute pet along with Penny, another girl who was all freckles and thin hair the color of wet sand. We were two kids who somehow got misplaced into their lives. Some-

KAREN J.
WEYANT

BIBLE DRILLS

23

times, when they walked by us, they merely patted us on our heads, their long nails tapping our skin.

Penny ducked their fingers. "They are like my sisters," she sniffed, clearly not impressed.

But I didn't mind. I wanted their attention. Back home, I was easily lost as the youngest in a family of eight, and my older sisters had moved out long ago. They were married and raising children, clearly leaving the rebellious life of a teenager behind. Instead, I had brothers and neighborhood boys who were ready for rough and tumble play and little else.

So, I tried to look like them. I tied my T-shirts into single knots that rested just above my belt line. I tried to fluff my bangs into soft spikes off my forehead. I begged my mother for rubber bracelets, made famous by Madonna, and a Benetton sweatshirt left at home, to be sent in a care package. When they did indeed come in the mail, I wore them proudly.

Their response? Faint, amused smiles. I may have received another pat on the head.

I was doomed to be a mere pet for the summer.

But that changed the night of the Bible drill.

Bible drills were contests held between bunkhouses. The preacher would stand in front of the Chapel pews and give a Bible reference. Then, with Bibles in our hands, we would scramble to find the verse, the tissue thin paper of both the New and Old Testaments, almost ripping in a flurry of fingers. Some verses were easier to find—anything in Genesis or Matthew, for example. Other verses were much more difficult. For instance, who really remembered where the book of Nahum was? Or Ruth? And yes, while all of us knew the story of Jonah and the Whale, who could readily fumble through the Old Testament to find the actual book of Jonah?

A key perk was that if one knew the verse, he or she could stand up without finding it in their Bible, and recite the words. This, of course, was a benefit to their team because if recited correctly, they instantly got the point.

However, many kids either did not memorize verses in their home Sunday school classes, or the tension of those contests made them forget any past knowledge, for very few braved this strategy.

That night, we were losing. In last place, we had few points, all won by Penny who was the fastest in our bunkhouse. I felt the frustration mounting through the hard, wooden pews.

"Psalm 23:1," said the Preacher in a calm voice.

All around me, pages flicked as if the Bibles were frantically whispering among themselves. But I paused.

"Psalm 23:1?" I thought to myself. "I know that verse."

I glanced around me. Everyone was intent on finding the verse in their Bibles. No one seemed to realize the commonplace of Psalm 23:1.

I stood up, and in a shaky voice, recited the whole verse in its simplicity. "The Lord is my Shepherd, I shall not want."

Pages stopped turning, as hundreds of eyes started at me. Floorboards creaked, and everyone seemed to hold their breath. In my memory, even the night insects outside grew silent, although I am sure that didn't happen.

For a moment I waited. Maybe I had the wrong verse?

But I had been so sure, so very sure.

Then, the preacher smiled and nodded, giving our team the point.

There was no cheering. We were, after all, in a chapel, a place of worship, but there was clapping, and smiles, and most of all Roxanne, who was wearing a single silver hoop reached over to pull me next to her.

We didn't win that Bible drill, but we also didn't come in last place. And, in the days that would follow, the girls would make room for me at meal times. They would show me how to tame my frizzy hair into a wavy ponytail. They would teach me how to mix lipstick with chapstick for a soft, demure color and how to wear blush and foundation that would mask my sunburned cheeks.

But at that moment in the chapel, I didn't yet know that these lessons would come. As I sat close, I breathed in Roxanne's deodorant and perfume. We sang the last hymn for the night. Then, we all bowed our heads in prayer, except for me. I glanced over at Roxanne, her eyes closed, and watched how the light danced through her one silver earring.

25

SOLIDAGO
JOURNAL

WINTER 2018

INITIATION

PHIL
NIPPERT

**CITYSCAPE
WITH
BRIDGE CONTOUR
STUDY**

27

SOLIDAGO
JOURNAL

WINTER 2018

INITIATION

PHIL
NIPPERT

GIANT OAK

29

SOLIDAGO
JOURNAL

WINTER 2018

INITIATION

PHIL
NIPPERT

ZINNIAS

31

SOLIDAGO
JOURNAL

WINTER 2018

INITIATION

JIM
ZOLA

UNTITLED #9

33

SOLIDAGO
JOURNAL

WINTER 2018

INITIATION

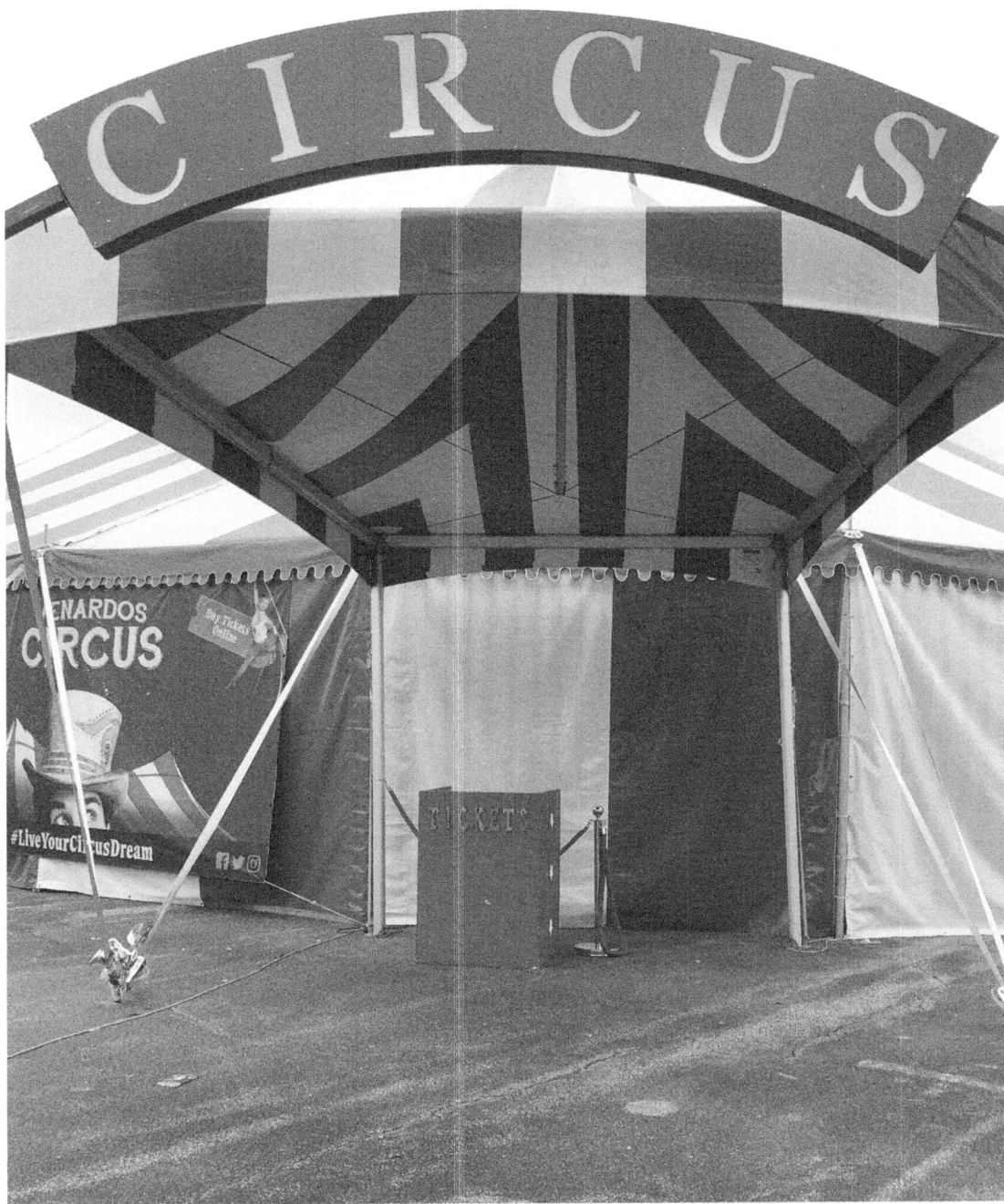

STACY
YELTON

**WAITING
FOR THE
BARKER**

35

SOLIDAGO
JOURNAL

WINTER 2018

INITIATION

Ignore what you have heard.
Do not ford these waters,
do not walk these shores.
Stab the door of your house shut with rail spikes,
and admit no messenger
who speaks with our accent.

Drop a bomb on us,
declare us quarantined.
Tell them what you have to:
say our air is haunted,
say our soil is sick with devils.

When, despite my words,
you find yourself residing here,
go as long as you can
without tasting our food,
and remember: nobody knows
what they're laughing at.

Now, roll this up,
put it back into the bottle,
return it to the water,
and cut your hands off at the wrists.

ART
ZILLERUELO

**IF YOU ARE
READING THIS,
THE BOTTLE
MADE IT ACROSS**

SOLIDAGO
JOURNAL

WINTER 2018

INITIATION

Jenna singsongs her way to the lake, "Tip my boat, I'll still float." She isn't rushing, but her small footsteps are quicker than mine.

"That canoe better not flip!"

"But you'd still float." Her laughter sparkles like wine, these meager sun-tipped waves, this summer day.

I don't want to admonish her; my tongue rubs against my teeth until I find an easy line. "Only because I put on my life jacket." We reach the water's edge. "Otherwise I'd plummet to the bottom like a rock."

"What does plummet mean?"

"Fall really fast." I hold the vessel steady for her to crawl over the edge. "Or maybe it's a small bird." I hand her our sack lunch, then the fishing poles. She dutifully places them in their customary spots before taking her seat. I untie the rope, push the canoe from the wedge it has created in the clay from frequent trips in and out of our small harbor this season.

"Do you plummet in love?" Jenna asks when I climb aboard and settle in to row.

"I never thought about it, but I guess you could."

"No." Her mouth is all apout. "Do you?"

I think about all the things I had hoped to impart to my niece over this summer: How to be brave, trust her gut, resist the vultures in whatever field she pursues. Instead, she's heard about crushes and is interested in the parameters of love.

I tell her the truth. "I did once."

"With Uncle Steven?"

"No. It was a long time ago."

She picks up her pole, casts it into the water earlier than I would have suggested. "Who was it with?"

"Just a boy," I say. *Just the perfect man.*

T.L.
SHERWOOD

**THE ONE
THAT GOT AWAY**

"What happened to him?"

I anchor the oars in place. "I don't know. We lost touch."

"How come? I mean, you *plummeted* in love with him."

I summon up a weak smile. "I guess we weren't right for each other." She's quiet for a while and I'm grateful. In my youth, I hated the half-answers I got from my aunts - hate that I'm repeating this extended family pattern. I cast my own line. "Actually, I do know. He lives far away and has a beautiful lawyer wife and three baby girls."

When the fishing gets frustrating, Jenna opens the sack, hands me my beer then opens her diet cola. "Do you think you'll ever see him again?"

"No!" I inhale, startled by my abrupt response. I bite my lower lip, whisper, "I mean, I don't want to."

She waits three beats, checks her line. " 'Cuz the plummet left marks?"

I nearly laugh. "I'm going to miss you, kid."

"I'm not a kid."

Bobbing my head, I say, "I know."

"And you don't have to move to Japan to be a translator. Mom said you could work in Washington or Seattle or even New York City if you wanted to."

I'm silent in her rebuke. Saying, "I know," won't add to this conversation.

She says, "You know, when I plummet in love, I'm going to grab hold of that girl and take her with me, all the way down to the end of the ocean."

I admire my niece's temerity, her devotion to easy answers, that her semi-sheltered life has been devoid of real conflict or unresolved issues. I stare out at the musty blue hills in the distance and ask, "But what if she floats?"

"What?" She sniggers. "Like a bird?" Jenna leans back and grins. "Then we'll soar."

SOLIDAGO
JOURNAL

WINTER 2018

INITIATION

And so twilight comes
To us all
A softening of days
Knees no longer spry
Mind forgetful
Eyes clouding and weary

Our calling at ebb:
Stapling papers
At a desk
Waiting for the watch
The fishing pole

The sun's rotation
Out of our hands
Sinking to shadow
As vesper tolls
And rays scatter
Before dark
Like children at play

Best to view twilight
From across the river
With artist's eye
Praise the birches

ALLISON
THORPE

**POINT OF VIEW,
WITH BIRCHES**

SOLIDAGO
JOURNAL

WINTER 2018

INITIATION

Spencer was leaving his wife, Cassandra, and their two children, Melody and Levi. Melody was twelve, chocolate-haired, and accomplished on the violin. Her favorite color was mauve, and she found eggs, scrambled or otherwise, revolting. Spencer felt confident that Melody was the sort of girl who'd be prudent and prudish, at least until she was legal. Levi was blond and seven, toothy and not too sharp, bewitched by trucks and trains, transportation in general, as well as ice cream, which he could never manage, whether it came in a cup or cone. Cassandra, well. She was busy. Eternally occupied, rushing, thinking, scratching out and scratching through ballpoint lists, staring off into a place in space that was composed of dental appointments and vaccinations and re-upholstery. But still, in all the ways that seemed to matter to everyone else, Cassandra was near perfect. He knew it. She knew it. But none of that mattered. Spencer was leaving them, all three of them, with the two-storey brick in the good school district so he could move into a one-bedroom apartment in the bad one.

What difference did it make where he lived? It wasn't like he was going to school. He didn't need a science lab that promised no less than one microscope per two students. He wasn't going to get remarried and have more kids who he felt deserved a cap on class size or a cafeteria that composted or a jazz band elective. A one-bedroom that backed up to the reservoir, to a chain-link fence woven with windblown grocery sacks, was all that Spencer required. That and a leather couch and a mattress on cinder blocks and a premiere cable package and a couple of bars of Zest.

Spencer had no use for a plaster bird bath or matching nightstands with brass claw-and-ball feet or a toile camelback sofa like the one he'd been living with for fifteen years. It wasn't like he'd miss the salmon bath towels that advertised *CFW* (her initals, not his) or the tissue box made of mother of pearl that held little more than something he was going to snot on. And he could certainly do without the carp-shaped windsock and the perky pineapple flag and Cassandra's "Melody has a tap recital and Levi has a soccer banquet and don't forget that next weekend we promised to go see so-and-so who just gave birth to such-and-such." Spencer was just fine making that whole song-and-dance go away. The sheer madness of self-made madness had just become more than he could bear. So, Spencer had made up his mind to leave. All he wanted now was to run the numbers all day and come home at 6.45 to an empty apartment that smelled of old, sculpted shag. He wanted to walk in the door with his Mexican carryout and sit on the couch and watch *Bonanza Gold Diggers* and eat queso and chips and drink warm, dark, Irish beer.

This was an image he played in his mind, on loop, as if it were pornography. He knew he was imagining the classic divorced man, the dead-beat dad. He knew it should bring him some sort of guilt or grief or horror, but all it brought him was relief. When he saw himself on the couch, getting fat, the cheese down the front of his button-down, the dingy walls where someone else's picture hooks still hung, the television on while he slept in his work clothes, beer tipping invisible into the deep shag, it was like a little window into Eden. He could hear the angels sing.

* * *

Of course, everyone wanted to know why Spencer was leaving. Was there someone else? Was he going broke? Had he lost his job months back? Had he been pretending to go to work all this time while he was really going to a bar all day to drink? Was it pain pills? Was he secretly dying? Was he finally coming out of the closet? The answer was always the same: no, no, no, no, no, no, no.

"Men," his boss informed him, "never leave unless they have a plan. And by 'plan' I mean 'woman.'" But Spencer didn't have a woman. His lover was emptiness. He had nothing outside of his marriage. He had nothing inside of himself. It was as if he'd been erased, hosed down. He knew he loved Cassandra and Melody and Levi, but he couldn't feel it. He knew nothing other than that feeling nothing was wrong. Spencer didn't know how to explain why he was leaving until one day, in counseling, with Cassandra sitting beside him dabbing at her swollen eyes, it came to him. "It's just," he paused, momentarily exhilarated that it had finally dawned on him. "It's just that life isn't what I thought it would be."

There was a brief moment of silence during which Spencer heard a woman laugh, far off, outside in the parking lot. Then Cassandra lurched from the couch, as if someone had stabbed her in the back. She nearly turned over the coffee table that held the Kleenex, the dish of Wint O Green mints, the grimy communal stress ball.

"Well," she said, trembling. "I've officially heard it all." Then she grabbed her purse and her coat and stormed out of the office in a puff of cold air that felt like a flash of death but dissipated soon enough. The therapist waited until she was gone, then he blew air out of his nose in a bullish way.

"Spencer," Dr. Darvin said. "Tell me some things that have turned out the way you expected."

Queso from Durango's, Spencer thought. *Bonanza Gold Diggers.* But Spencer did not say these things aloud.

"Life has a lot of moving parts," the doctor said. "But if we start from love instead of obligation, those parts can be a lot easier to manage."

That made Spencer think of the year he played baseball. He'd been ten. He liked the coach. He liked the teammates. He even liked the uniform, the feel of the ball tossed up and down in his glove, the sound of the bat when it made a good connection. But everything put together had seemed a joke. All the parts, when forced to interact, seemed absurd. What was the point, this running from here to there? This line and that line? It was a fabrication. A farce. An orchestrated circus that caused grown men to turn crimson, women to scream nose-to-nose with other women, children to doubt their self-worth.

One particular May Saturday, after a missed triple, it even caused one man, an opposing coach with a handlebar mustache, to drop to his knees and clutch his heart. At first, it seemed a show, a dramatic reaction. Some of Spencer's teammates even pointed and jeered. But when the man keeled over on his forehead in the orange dirt and proceeded to foam at the mouth, it became clear something dire had come to pass. And all in the name of something made-up and make-believe.

An ambulance eventually came to cart him off, but by the time it arrived, bouncing over the grass, the coach was purple. Spencer watched the EMTs bend over the man, their green latex gloves perched on their hips like exotic birds. He watched them lift the man's limp body onto a stretcher. He watched the ambulance retreat. People stood in the warm sun and murmured. Spencer squinted into the sky until he felt nothing. Then he took off his glove and took off his hat and went to retrieve his bat, until his coach grabbed his elbow and frowned. "The game goes on, Spencer," he said. It always goes on." And it did. With the same, if not intensified, passion as before.

Spencer wondered if that was when his heart had gone blank, when that opposing coach had foamed his way to indigo. Sure, Spencer had mustered enough emotion in his later years to court Cassandra the way most actuaries courted, and to propose to Cassandra the way most actuaries proposed, but when things had gotten tough, when the family pandemonium had begun, he'd reverted to squinting into the sky and erasing himself. When his children presented him with frustrating scenarios, when Cassandra laid out her to-do lists on the dining room table, one-two-three-four-five, Spencer could feel apathy coming on like a trance, like a squeegee down a plate glass window. That was when he went through the motions of pretending to care, of pretending to be interested, when what he really wondered was what would life be like if no one pretended to be interested, when what he really wondered was what would life be like if no one did anything. If everyone just got on the floor and curled up together and only rose to use the toilet and to make instant oatmeal. Spencer thought for a moment about voicing this to Dr. Darvin, but instead, he just sat there on the gray couch and thought of the sofa back at the two-storey. What had those people on the fabric been doing? He'd stared at them for years while Cassandra sat by his side, with her ballpoint and lists, but now he couldn't recall what those people printed all over the camelback had been up to. Fishing, maybe. Threshing wheat. Spencer couldn't recall and it hurt to try. So, he stood up, helped himself to some Wint O Greens, put on his hat, and tipped it.

* * *

Spencer thought that going back to the house to say goodbye and pack up his things would be hard on the kids. He felt like it would be a big event, a dramatic exit. So he left the clothes and the kids and Cassandra the same way he left cocktail parties--without saying "so long" or "thank you." He just went to work one morning and didn't go back home when he was done. On the way to his new apartment, he bought a bar of Zest and a cheap yellow toothbrush and he left everything else back at the two-storey. He figured it was thoughtful of him in a way, Cassandra and the kids could slowly get used to him not being there, and then when they got used to that, maybe toward summer, they could go through his closet and empty it out and get used to his clothes not being there either. What else had he really left behind besides some oxfords and khakis? His uncle's war helmet, he supposed. Maybe a set of damp encyclopedias in the basement. A box of Wheat Thins. (He was the only one who ate Wheat Thins.) It wasn't like it was hard to start over. He just needed some basics. Some socks and paper plates. A container of Coffee Mate. Batteries for the remote.

* * *

Spencer's friends thought he was crazy. They told his as much. Cassandra looked good for her age. She wasn't more than 130, 135 in the winter. Once or twice a month, she could be a real pill, a borderline bitch, but the rest of the time she was a doll, sometimes a saint. She had good teeth, a genuine laugh, a way of anticipating the needs of the kids. She still gave it up every

week or so, usually in a tired sort of way, but she acquiesced nonetheless. And the kids weren't terrors. They had manners enough, a modicum of charm.

"You've lost your mind," Bill said.

"Really, Spencer," Mike said. "What more could you want?"

Spencer saw the queso and chips. He saw Pearson brothers on Channel 241 running Klondike gravel through their sluice box. He also saw no talking. No folded laundry in the front hall. No obligation to expain the rules of badminton, *Clue*, the foxtrot, geometry. He saw himself never having to show someone how to ride a ten-speed, how to wind up a rubber hose, how to measure twice, cut once. Never again would he want to put his fist through a wall watching Levi tie his shoes by clumping his shoelaces up in a little pile. Never again would he experience the agony of seeing that nightly lump of toothpaste in Melody's sink. *Did she just let it fall there off her toothbrush? Did she spit it out whole? How much had he spent on these lumps?* Spencer knew it was wrong. There were people out there who had kids dying. Kids hooked up to tubes and bags and pumps. But still: a scooter left behind the wheel of his Camry three or four times a week. It was just one thing after another.

* * *

On the first morning in the new apartment, Spencer looked out at the chain-link and stretched. He didn't feel anything. Neither remorseful nor refreshed. He just felt nothing. Which was how he wanted it. Before it had always been something.

At work, he ran some numbers, then he had a piece of cake in the break room, then he ran some more numbers. When he went back for a second piece of cake, he ran into Babson, the IT guy, doing the same.

"Good cake," Babson said. "I think it's spice. No one ever makes spice cake anymore."

Spencer just chewed and gave a nod.

"Hey, sorry," Babson said. "About everything going on." He brushed some crumbs from one hand onto the knees of his pants. "I heard around."

Spencer wasn't sure what to say, so he said, "Well. Life's no picnic."

Babson crossed his arms and nodded. "You got that right," he said.

49

"Even a picnic is no picnic. The last time I went on a picnic, I..." Babson trailed off.

"What?" Spencer said.

Babson looked as if he's been caught reaching for a third piece of cake. "Oh, nothing," he said. "I don't know what I was going to say."

Spencer suddenly felt persistent, almost pushy. "No. You were going to tell me something. Come on. Tell me. Tell a man a story."

Babson raised his shoulders and shook his head. "It's really not that great of a story," he said. "I just came across an animal is all."

Babson paused and Spencer stared. He stared in a way intended to make Babson feel obligated. Spencer knew it was out of character for him to act as such. It was the first time he was using his predicament to garner pity, to force a reaction. "What kind of animal, Babson?" Spencer asked. He surprised himself by calling Babson by name. He surprised Babson too.

"It was a cat," Babson said quietly. "Tangled in some wire."

Spencer felt something in him lighten. "Like barbed wire?"

Babson shrugged. "Yeah," he said. "I tried to get him out, but it just made things worse." Babson uncrossed his arms, rubbed his neck. Then he clasped his hands behind him.

"So," Spencer said. "Then what?"

Babson cleared his throat. "I had no choice," he said. "I put it out of its misery."

Spencer held his cake a little higher, intrigued. "Really?" he said. "Good for you." Babson gave a weak smile. "And how did you do that?" Spencer asked. "How does one go about putting a cat out of its misery?"

Babson looked at the floor, then out the glass door of the break room. He moved in front of the door to block it. "I had no choice," he said again, almost whispering. "It was the right thing to do."

Spenser stood in a way that he normally didn't stand. Unyielding, feet slightly apart, one hand speared in a pocket, the other, paused indefinitely,

with the cake out in front of him. It was a stance that made it clear Babson was going nowhere until he told Spencer how he killed the cat. Babson looked over his shoulder and out the glass door then back at Spencer. "I didn't have anything on me," he said. There was a long pause before Babson spoke again. "It was a picnic, for chrissakes. All I had was a corkscrew."

Spenser stared at Babson for a second to let it sink in. Then he resumed eating his square of spice cake. "Hmph," he said with his mouth full. "Wowf."

Babson ran his fingers through his hair. "I don't know why you brought all this up," he said. "I think I was just trying to make a point, you know. That nothing ever goes perfect in life. Not even a picnic."

Spencer finished his cake. He saw the cat as calico in his mind. He didn't know why, but he felt certain it was a calico. He thought he might ask Babson what the cat looked like, but then he moved past him in a friendly way and said: "Well. Back to work."

* * *

That night, back at the apartment, Spencer kept thinking about the cat. He couldn't focus on his television program or his queso, not even his Irish beer, just the calico in the barbed wire. Before he fell asleep, Spencer made up his mind to go on a picnic. He'd go Saturday, first thing. March wasn't quite picnicking season, but he had his mind set on it. His hope was that he would come across something like Babson had come across. Something that required either saving or slaying. Spencer considered the various ways this could happen: a dog in a well, a duck wrapped in some discarded fishing line, a deer with its legs caught in an old cattle gate. Any of those would suffice.

* * *

Saturday was cold and royal blue. Spencer woke and dressed in a new pair of jeans and a new gray sweatshirt and a new jacket that featured a little icon of a basketball player dunking. Spencer had never been a basketball fan, but the jacket was something that he could buy now that he didn't live with people who would ask him why he'd bought it. He made a cup of instant coffee and while he drank it, he watched the grocery bags in the fence flap in the breeze. Then he went to the nice grocery, the gourmet one that sold baskets and macaroons and French cheese, and he bought a basket and macaroons and French cheese. He also bought wine. And a corkscrew. When all that was done, he drove thirty miles out of town until he came to a large swath of land that was maybe part of someone's farm, maybe government land.

Spencer left his car on the gravel shoulder. He climbed over the guardrail and over a fence and he walked until he came to a meadow of dry winter grass tucked between two long stands of walnut and cedar. He spread out his basketball jacket and sat on it. He broke off some of the cheese. He ate a few macaroons. He opened the wine and drank straight from the bottle. He tried to figure out a way to balance the bottle without it tipping over, but it was too precarious, so he had no choice but to drink it all. After a while, he lay back and closed his eyes. It was cold, but he tried to imagine what kind of animal he might come across in a plain place like this. Maybe a coyote or dairy cow. Maybe a hawk dragging a broken wing. Spencer went in and out of sleep. He felt he was attached to a balloon. He felt he was lodged in a deep crack in the earth. He felt he could not remember his name. Then something came into view. It was the toile camelback couch from the two-storey. There in the cold field in his half sleep, he saw what the people printed on it were doing. It was a story. Of a family. Of a woman with apples in her lifted apron. Of two children, a girl tying ribbons in a pony's mane, a boy sailing a boat with some sort of stick. There was also a man, leaning against a towering elm and playing a flute. It was the sort of world where the father might go out into the world, smiling and properly dressed, and buy his children something. A ball, a kite, or better yet, a cat. It was the sort of sunlit universe where there was little to do. Where the wind never rose above a breeze. Where a husband might show up on his old doorstep and press the doorbell and present his family with a kitten. It was a world where nothing had to be explained. Gifts could just be presented and the presenter could stay or leave. There were no obligations.

At this, Spencer woke fully. He sat up and looked around. The sky was no longer blue but white. He gathered the empty bottle and the corkscrew, the tin of macaroons, what was left of the cheese. He put the things back in the basket. He stood and put on his jacket. Then he walked out of the field and up to a small hill. In one direction, he could see his car, in the other he could see where he had just been. He closed his eyes and saw himself buying the cat. He saw himself ringing the doorbell. He saw himself handing the cat to Melody and Levi. He saw their joy and Cassandra's sorrow. Then he saw himself leaving. He saw himself leave again and again, over and over. Going from his old house to his new couch until, it too, was completely worn out.

SOLIDAGO
JOURNAL

WINTER 2018

INITIATION

On my last day of college, a dean stopped me on my way out of the cafeteria during lunch to congratulate me. He and I had had conflicts over college policies during my years there, and I'd always assumed he wasn't fond of me, but running into him then, he seemed genuinely happy for me. He smiled and hugged me and said "We've had our ups and downs here, all of us, but it's a learning process. Always a learning process." I said "Thank you," and walked out of the cafeteria and down a hill to the library. I tried to read, but the library was so empty, and so full of memories for me. I felt panicky and mournful. The part of my life where I read here was over. I left.

A month later, the dean's son, not too much older than me, killed himself. When I found this out, I was working two jobs, one at a job search help lab at the public library, the other at a restaurant and bar. I'd heard his son had died soon after it happened, but it wasn't until months later, over pizza and beer with one of my former professors, that I'd learned it was a suicide.

"He had a fiancée," my professor said. "It's just sad."

How the subject came up I can't remember. Over drinks our conversations ranged from the new anti-depressants I was taking to the Beat Generation poets to my post-college what-do-I-do-next terror. Years later, we would date, and I would find out that he was an alcoholic, and he would yell at me until I cried, but now, before all that, I only saw his good side.

"I'm afraid I won't find friends like I had in college if I leave here," I told him.

"People are the same everywhere, L," he said. "Just go. It's easy."

"No, it's not. There's money and finding work and missing people who are far away."

"No, it's easy. Easy."

Three weeks later, I quit my job at the restaurant. Working on my feet and lifting boxes of beer had brought back joint pain that started in high school and that I thought had finally gone away for good. My wrists burned. My knees ached. I couldn't walk on the ankle I'd sprained when I'd fallen through the floor of an attic three years prior. My father told me he would help me with money and if the pain was that bad, I could quit. So I did and felt like a failure—weak and fragile. My professor and future lover was wrong. How could I

L. DAVIS

A LEARNING
EXPERIENCE

55

move away if I couldn't even work? So my last day of work came, and though I had dreaded it, it ended up being a pleasant evening. After I mopped the floor for the last time, wrapped up the unused meat from the kitchen for the last time, scrubbed the sinks smelling of seafood for the last time, my boss gave me a free beer. I sat outside in the warm night with my coworkers, one of whom shared a bite of her cheesecake with me. Another gave me a cigarette, and someone pointed out that it was almost midnight, but there was a man who had jogged by the restaurant three times now and that sent me into a giggle fit, the kind that I can't stop, and soon everyone was laughing at that, and I felt happy and appreciated and grateful.

"By the way," my boss said to one of the cooks, "the friend Oreos were horrible today. You used too much batter."

"Sorry, bossman," the cook replied. "I'm really sorry. I don't know what happened."

My boss smiled. "It's okay," he said. "It's all a learning experience. It's okay to make mistakes. That's how you learn."

I found out the next day that while I was laughing with my coworkers at the restaurant, one of my best friends was having one of the worst nights of her life. A friend of hers had fallen to his death while hiking. He was 21, and his death, to me, proved that our lives are accidents. I obsessed over it, wondering if he felt pain, if he felt fear. I had barely known him. We had exchanged brief words at a New Year's Eve party six months ago. I Googled his obituary, news articles about his death. I Googled photos of him and his friends, his family. I browsed his Twitter account, as if looking for a sign that he knew he only had a little time left, that he was ready to leave. Things that near strangers shouldn't do. I started jolting awake while sleeping, the thought "He's dead, he's dead" flashing through my mind. I imagined what his mother was feeling, and I knew I could never imagine. I wondered what she would think if someone told her it was a learning experience. I wondered what anything I've ever learned will mean when I'm dead.

His death reminded me of a story a coworker had told me in college. I was working on campus as an electrician's helper for the summer, and while we went about rewiring one of the faculty houses, somehow my coworker got on the subject of a girl who had lived down the street from him when he was growing up.

"She was in high school, had this boyfriend. They broke up, so she turned her parents' car on in the closed garage. She was being dramatic, obviously, and probably didn't want to die, but she had asthma and had an attack and died. I had a lot of dreams about her after that."

We didn't talk anymore about the girl. I've always seen a certain nobility in some forms of death. A person lives a good life and fights until the end and when they pass from old age or cancer or some other ailment, their family mourns and celebrates their life. But this girl in her parents' car seemed so pointless. She'd made a mistake, but learned nothing. Maybe nobility was just luck. And when I started to think like this, I felt a darkness come over my mind.

Quitting my job didn't help. I saw multiple doctors: two orthopedists, both of whom gave me cortisone injections in my ankles, which did nothing, and then announced that they didn't know what was wrong; a new primary care doctor who was also stumped; a rheumatologist who was very sympathetic and listened to me, but could give me no answers. I was tested for arthritis, lupus, vitamin deficiencies. I had x-rays and MRIs and blood tests and cried in the rheumo's office when she told me that everything looked normal. I wanted a diagnosis, a name for my ailment, even if it was something incurable. At least then there would be a reason for my pain, a tidy name to put on my suffering, something people could understand and accept.

Depression was a cause of pain with a name, and in addition to my physical pain, that emotional pain had come back in full force since I left college. It had been a part of my life since childhood, when I had cried at night, every night, when my mother took me to therapy when I was only seven. My primary care doctor said depression can cause physical pain, and I became preoccupied with this, wondering what I could change to heal myself. I had anger toward myself that continued to grow. It was my fault, all my fault. College had kept me busy, but now, graduated, with only my part-time library job, I worked, came home, drank, slept a lot, sinking down, down, down, and the further I went, the harder it was to see a way out.

In the summer, I got back together with a guy I had dated earlier in the year, and soon after we started sleeping together again, I got a yeast infection. I was able to treat it at home, but once he and I slept together again, it would come back, and because I couldn't say no to being wanted, I decided to put up with the discomfort until he moved to California the next month.

57

Once he moved, though, I couldn't get the infection to cease. I tried over-the-counter medicines and home remedies like yoghurt and garlic. I finally went to a gynecologist, who gave me prescription cream. When that didn't work, the gynecologist told me to try it again, and when it failed to work again, she told me I shouldn't have used yoghurt, that I must have irritated something, and gave me a steroid cream that did absolutely nothing. I found a new gynecologist, who told me he saw no signs of infection, and sent me to a specialist in the next town over. There was a three month wait list. So I waited. By this point my joint pain and the discomfort of whatever gynecological disease I was suffering from—I could no longer wear underwear because it created the prickly sensation of a porcupine living in my pants—plus my loneliness, my lack of direction, my dissatisfaction with my life after college, made my depression symptoms worse than they'd been in years. I would call my father and say I felt hopeless, that life is just luck, that there was no point, and he told me I have to find small reasons to keep going, things like love for my family, or just the joy of a nice day or of laughing so hard it hurts or of a good meal with a glass of wine and homemade dessert, but I couldn't stop thinking about the boy who had fallen to his death, how he made one little mistake, maybe stepped on a loose rock, and then he was gone.

Three months after I quit the restaurant, my boss texted me.

"Hi, stranger. Just thinking of you. Want to come by sometime for drinks?"

I imagined reliving my last night at the restaurant, sitting outside with free beer and a cigarette, laughing, the kind of moment that my father insisted I needed to focus on, so I said yes, I would come by for a drink. That Friday night, I drove to the restaurant after closing time, expecting my coworkers to be almost finished closing down, but when I arrived, the only person who has there was my former boss. I had a bad feeling in my gut, but I went in anyway, deciding to make a run for it if he tried anything inappropriate.

My former boss was not an unattractive man, just much older than me and a little pudgy. He was married, and I had met his wife on a few occasions. She was pleasant, but I never saw her smile, and I always felt a little bad for her. Her husband spent upwards of eighty hours a week at his restaurant, and some nights when we closed, instead of going home to his family, he would stay and hang out with us, his face turning red as he drank more wine. He had already had one child, and while I worked for him, he had another. He was

always happy to see his kids when their mother brought them by the restaurant, but I imagined he was a distant father, always at the restaurant, like my father had been with work when I was little. My father was a physician, worked from seven to seven or later, and was often on-call during weekends: not a bad father, but one that was far away.

So I sat at the bar, and my former boss told me to pick out any beer I wanted, so I chose the banana bread beer, because I like the taste and it was low in alcohol. My strategy was to drink weak drinks, slowly, and after some conversation, scram, but I've always been a light-weight, and before long, the alcohol had relaxed me enough that I no longer felt awkward being there, alone, with my former boss who has a wife and two young children back home waiting for him.

He asked me about my life. I told him I wanted to go to library school in either Seattle of Montréal, that the joint pain that had caused me to quit working for him had yet to be cured or even receive a diagnosis. He told me how when his father died, he was in college. It changed everything for him, he said. He dropped out, hitchhiked, worked odd jobs around the country, smoked a lot of weed, and eventually came home and finished school. I figured he must have learned a lot doing all that, and I felt frail and stupid because I couldn't ever see myself venturing out so bravely.

I told him about how much I wanted to leave my hometown, but I was afraid. I couldn't even say of what. There was nothing tangible, just a general sense of dread and helplessness. I couldn't imagine going out on my own.

"We're all scared, L," he said to me. "Look at this restaurant for instance." I did look, at the beer bottles nested under fluorescent lights behind the bar, at the wine glasses dangling above our heads, the framed article from the time the local paper featured the restaurant and called it a huge success, on the far wall among signs advertising the brands of beer available. "It was a huge risk opening this. And a lot could still go wrong. But I gave it my best shot and so far it's working. And as long as you try, who can criticize you? You try, sometimes you fail, but you always learn."

I excused myself to take a bathroom break, and while peeing, I decided that I was enjoying our conversation. Maybe he wasn't being creepy. Maybe he really just wanted to talk.

Back at the bar, we started talking again. He showed me a cut on his leg from when he crashed his bike the week before, and I showed him a scar on my leg from when I crashed my bike in college. I pulled out my cellphone so I could check the time, at which point I noticed that I had a text message from my boss, sent only a few minutes ago, while I was in the bathroom.

"I feel comfortable saying this now. I really want to kiss you!!!" it read.

"Um, it's getting late. I have to go," I said, standing from the bar. I turned my back to him and immediately went for the door. Trying to pull it open, I discovered it was locked, and I began to panic. My boss came up behind me, pulled the keys from his pocket, and unlocked the door while saying "Well, glad you came by."

I got into my car without looking back. Back home, I laid on my bed and cried. I felt embarrassed, naïve. I should have known better. But I was crying for his wife, too. For everyone who can't trust the person who sleeps next to them. He sent me more text messages—a frowning face, "Is that bad?", "Well, fine.," "Thanks for coming by. Wish you were interested"—but I ignored them all until the next day: "Thanks for the beer and the life advice. Please don't ever contact me again."

* * *

The coming months brought me little improvement. There were countless visits to doctors, none of whom could tell me why I was in pain. I tried every home remedy I found on the internet: no sugar, no carbs, lots of water, stretches, and for my vaginal pain, garlic, aloe juice, some holistic suppository I got at the organic grocery store. Nothing helped, but trying to make it better took some of my anxiety away as I waited to see the specialist.

One day, I walked to the CVS down the street to buy baking soda. Another possible remedy, I had read, was to bathe in warm water and baking soda. Unlike the aloe juice and suppositories, baking soda was cheap, so I was in a good mood. I got in the checkout line and, glancing at the man behind me, noticed that he was carrying two bags of Funyuns. I don't remember deciding to talk to him. The words seemed just to come out of my mouth, probably because of my good mood.

"Oh, Funyuns," I said. "I used to eat those all the time when I was a kid. I can't stand them now."

"He gave me a brief smile. "It's for my wife. It's all she can eat now."

"Uh-huh," I said, not following.

"She's waiting out in the car. She's down to 97 pounds."

"Oh wow," I said, still not getting it.

"Yeah, cancer's a bitch."

I didn't know what to say.

"She's starting radiation tomorrow, and during that she won't be able to eat at all. She'll be using a tube. This should never have happened. There were two kinds of lasers available, but insurance wouldn't pay for the better one. So they gave her the cheap one, and it tore her all up inside. Had part of her colon removed. No bladder, no woman parts anymore. I asked the doctor why he didn't fight to get her the better treatment, and you know what he told me? He told me they have to draw the line somewhere. So now I'm about to lose my 55-year-old wife, and I don't know what to do, if I should take an AK47 and shoot up our HMO or what."

I was crying, and he was crying, and I hugged him, a total stranger in the CVS.

"It's okay, it's okay," he said, hugging me back, as if I was the one that needed comforting. "You're a sweet girl. It'll get better. Keep the faith."

I paid for my baking soda and left without looking back. During the walk home, I cried, and once I got home, I cried some more, face-down on my bed, into my pillow. After ten minutes or so, the sobbing passed, and I lay there, breathing, aching, not understanding.

* * *

Finally, in March, I saw the specialist and was diagnosed with vulvodynia, a chronic pain condition, and prescribed a lidocaine cream for temporary relief and physical therapy for permanent relief, which, the doctor assured me, should be very effective, but to think of being hopeful about any of my pain conditions made me anxious. I was expecting to hit another dead-end. The fact that my pain had a name is misleading, for not much is understood about what causes it or how to fix it, though pelvic floor therapy, which teaches the

61

muscles in my pelvis to relax, has seen the best results, so while driving home, I said thank you, to no-one in particular, for the small possibility that there was a way out of my pain.

Three days later, I received an e-mail from a literary journal telling me they wanted to publish an essay I had sent them, the first such I had ever received, and I cried and called my parents, my friends, my alcoholic professor I would later date, my boyfriend of the past month, and I allowed myself to feel hopeful.

Four days after that, I watched my mother try to rouse my father from the couch. He looked like he was sleeping, but his skin was too pale. She told me to call 911, and I did, but I stumbled over my words so my mother took the phone from me. I cried in the other room while my mother, my father's ex-wife of fourteen years and still one of his best friends, performed CPR to no effect. "My father is dead, my father is dead," I said to no one over and over again. My father had a history of depression and drug abuse. My father had killed himself.

The night after we found him, my boyfriend held me while I cried.

"I don't understand! I want my daddy back! I want my daddy back!"

"You don't have to understand," he said, stroking my hair. "Just breathe, just breathe."

I cried until I couldn't anymore.

"Breathe," he said. "Breathe. Breathe."

And I did.

WHITNEY COLLINS' fiction has appeared in *Grist, The Pinch, New Limestone Review, Pamplemousse, The Gateway Review, Shirley Magazine*, and *Lumina*. It is forthcoming in *Ninth Letter, Moon City Review*, and *The Laurel Review*. She received her MFA from Spalding University and lives in Lexington with her husband and sons.

AMANDA KELLEY CORBIN holds an MFA in fiction from the University of Kentucky and a BFA from Morehead State University. Her work has appeared in *Inscape, Kentucky Monthly's Writers' Showcase, JMMW, Eunonia Review, Fried Chicken and Coffee, American Book Review*, and *Madcap Review*, among others.

L. DAVIS lives in North Carolina with her husband and her dog.

SANDY DAVIS

HENRY GOLDKAMP has lived against the Mississippi his entire life. Recent work appears in *Cutbank, Xavier Review, glitterMOB, Permafrost, Notre Dame Review, The Cape Rock*, among others. Last year (2017) his work was nominated for a Pushcart and two Best of the Nets.

BAILEY MERLIN holds an MFA in fiction from Butler University. She has been published by *Chantwood Magazine, Drunk Monkeys, Streetlight Magazine, Into the Void, Crack the Spine*, among others. She writes in Boston, MA where she lives with 9-11 people (depending on the day), 2 cats, and 2 dogs. Find more of her work at baileymerlin.com.

PHIL NIPPERT graduated 1991 from Transylvania University, after majoring in Studio Arts. He didn't resume drawing and painting seriously again until 1999. He drew and sent away about 238 originals for Amnesty International's annual greeting cards to humanitarian activists from 2001 to 2011, with the idea that sending someone an original drawing is proof of time spent for just the recipient, even if they don't like the drawing or understand your language. Limited to being at home with chronic illness since mid-2017, he decided to start selling copies of works on paper online and started a website: www. masqualero.com. He is also on Etsy as "Scribbledruid." Phil has been a Darfur, Sudan activist and volunteer worker since 2007 (doing what he can from the US).

STEPHEN O'DONNELL has previously had short stories published in *The Bloody Key Society Periodical, Gambling the Aisle, Panoply*, and the *Avalon Literary Review* among others. He is currently working on his second novel.

T. L. SHERWOOD loves flash fiction, but hates flash floods. Her work appears or is forthcoming in *Spelk, Bending Genres, Former Cactus, New World Writing, On the Premises*, and *The Bacopa Review*. She's currently working on a novel and blogs twice a month at http://tlsherwood.wordpress.com/.

ALLISON THORPE is a poet from Lexington, KY. Her latest chapbook is *The Shepherds of Tenth Avenue* (forthcoming from Finishing Line Press). Recent work appears in *The Tipton Poetry Journal, Appalachian Heritage, Still: The Journal, Apex Magazine*, and *Apex Publications* anthology.

KAREN J. WEYANT's essays and poems have appeared in *Briar Cliff Review, Carbon Culture Review, cream city review, Chautauqua, Copper Nickel, Harpur Palate, Rattle, River Styx*, and *Whiskey Island*. She is the author of two chapbooks, including *Wearing Heels in the Rust Belt* published by Main Street Rag. She is an Associate Professor of English at Jamestown Community College in Jamestown, New York. In her spare time, she explores the Rust Belt regions of Western New York and Northern Pennsylvania.

STACY YELTON lives in Kentucky and takes several photographs every day. When the muse visits, she writes.

ART ZILLERUELO's poetry has appeared in *Hayden's Ferry Review, The Cincinnati Review, Pleiades, Western Humanities Review*, and other journals. His chapbook *Weird Vocation* was published by Kattywompus Press in 2015, and his book *The Last Map* was published by Unsolicited Press in 2017. He is Assistant Teaching Professor of English at Penn State Schuykill.

JIM ZOLA is a poet and photographer living in North Carolina.

www.solidagojournal.com

Made in the USA
Middletown, DE
01 April 2019